FANFARE

JON GEORGE

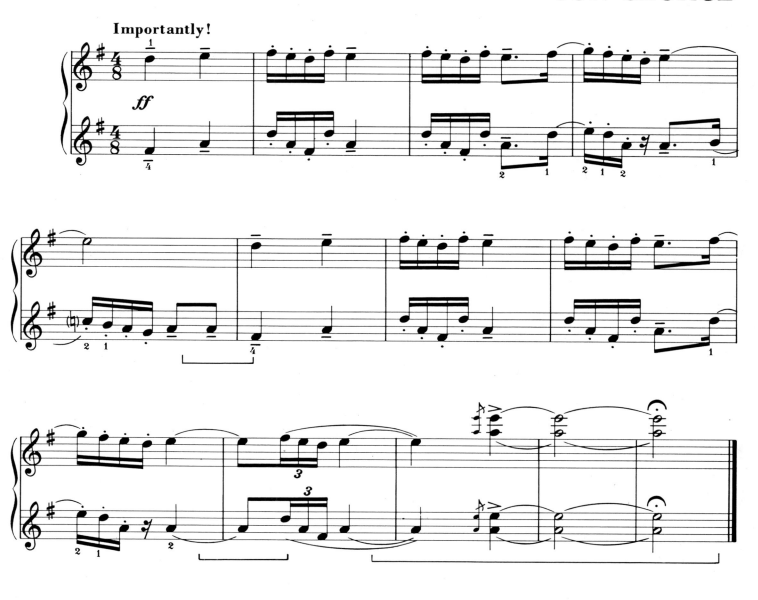

PROCESSIONAL

With great dignity

THE TOURNAMENT BEGINS

Everyone is anxiously awaiting the first event.

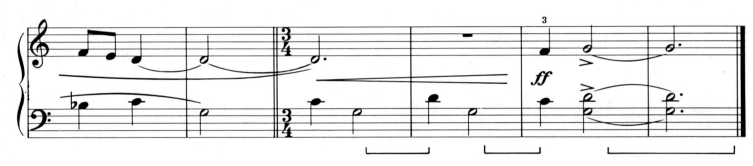

THE TROUBADOUR SINGS

"Once there was a Lady-in-Waiting; She did love a gallant Knight...."

THE JESTER PERFORMS

He has the king roaring with laughter!

Look! he even does cartwheels!

MINIATURE SUITE
1. BRANLE

Crisply, with precise articulation

poco rit.

2. AIR

With sweet melancholy

3. GIGGE

As fast as can be!

ISBN 978-0-19-385488-8